JUL 14 2017

610-L

D1060836

North Palm Beach Library

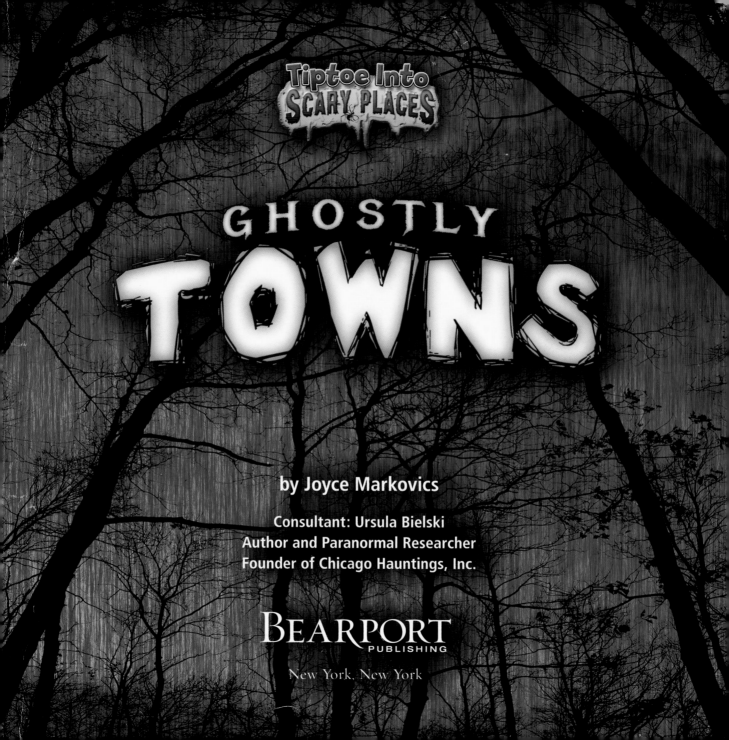

Tiptoe Into
SCARY PLACES

GHOSTLY TOWNS

by Joyce Markovics

Consultant: Ursula Bielski
Author and Paranormal Researcher
Founder of Chicago Hauntings, Inc.

BEARPORT
PUBLISHING

New York, New York

Credits

Cover, Kim Jones; TOC, © Stan de Haas Photography/Shutterstock, © carlosobriganti/Shutterstock, and © SCOTTCHAN/Shutterstock; 4–5, © Atmosphere1/Shutterstock and © Mariusz S. Jurgielewicz/Shutterstock; 6, © Lukas Gojda/Shutterstock; 7, © Carver Mostardi/Alamy; 7TR, © ZUMA Press, Inc./Alamy; 8L, © James Schaedig/Alamy and © andras_csontos/Shutterstock; 8R, © Taylor Hinton/iStock; 9, © ZUMA Press, Inc./Alamy; 10–11, © Rob Crandall/Shutterstock; 11TL, Public Domain; 11TR, © Smit/Shutterstock; 12L, © Zack Frank/Shutterstock; 12R, © Photo #557, Bud Moore Papers, Archives and Special Collections, Mansfield Library, University of Montana-Missoula; 13, © Konstantin32/Dreamstime; 14, © North Wind Picture Archives/Alamy; 15, © Alan J Jones/Alamy; 16, © Universal History Archive/UIG/Bridgeman Images; 17, © Captblack76/Shutterstock; 18, W.N. Manning/Public Domain; 19, © Stephen Saks Photography/Alamy; 20–21, © vitmore/Shutterstock; 23, © Steven Castro/Shutterstock.

Publisher: Kenn Goin
Senior Editor: Joyce Tavolacci
Creative Director: Spencer Brinker
Photo Researcher: Thomas Persano
Cover: Kim Jones

Library of Congress Cataloging-in-Publication Data

Names: Markovics, Joyce L., author.
Title: Ghostly towns / by Joyce Markovics.
Description: New York, New York : Bearport Publishing, [2017] | Series:
  Tiptoe into scary places | Audience: Ages 5–8. | Includes bibliographical
  references and index.
Identifiers: LCCN 2016037732 (print) | LCCN 2016038410 (ebook) | ISBN
  9781684020515 (library) | ISBN 9781684021031 (ebook)
Subjects: LCSH: Ghost towns—Juvenile literature. | Cities and
  towns—Legends—Juvenile literature. | Haunted places—Juvenile literature.
Classification: LCC BF1461 .M3575 2017 (print) | LCC BF1461 (ebook) | DDC
  133.1/22—dc23
LC record available at https://lccn.loc.gov/2016037732

Copyright © 2017 Bearport Publishing Company, Inc. All rights reserved. No part of this publication may be reproduced in whole or in part, stored in any retrieval system, or transmitted in any form or by any means, electronic, mechanical, photocopying, recording, or otherwise, without written permission from the publisher.

For more information, write to Bearport Publishing Company, Inc., 45 West 21st Street, Suite 3B, New York, New York 10010. Printed in the United States of America.

10 9 8 7 6 5 4 3 2 1

CONTENTS

GHOSTLY TOWNS

You see crumbling buildings swallowed by weeds. Shards of glass jut out of empty windows. The wind whips up a cloud of dust. There isn't a soul in sight. Then why does it feel like someone is watching you? Could someone—or something— be living in this eerie town forgotten by time?

4

Get ready to read four haunting tales about ghostly towns. Turn the page . . . if you have the nerve!

Forever in Flames

Centralia, Pennsylvania

Centralia was once a busy mining town. Now, it's silent and **deserted**. Why? A mysterious fire has been burning there for fifty years.

In 1962, a fire was started in the town dump. The blaze silently spread belowground. It caused the coal in nearby underground mines to burst into flames.

A deserted road in Centralia, Pennsylvania

An empty home in Centralia

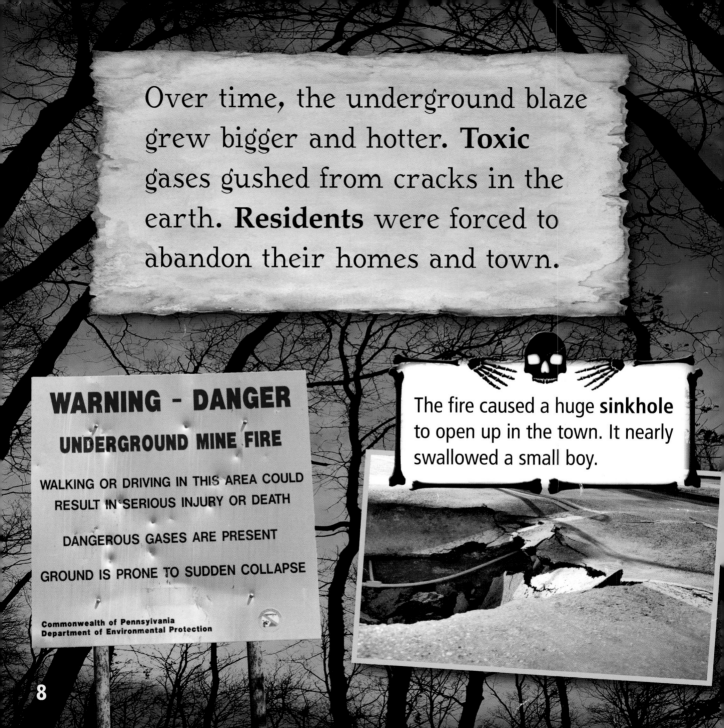

Over time, the underground blaze grew bigger and hotter. **Toxic** gases gushed from cracks in the earth. **Residents** were forced to abandon their homes and town.

WARNING - DANGER

UNDERGROUND MINE FIRE

WALKING OR DRIVING IN THIS AREA COULD RESULT IN SERIOUS INJURY OR DEATH

DANGEROUS GASES ARE PRESENT

GROUND IS PRONE TO SUDDEN COLLAPSE

Commonwealth of Pennsylvania
Department of Environmental Protection

The fire caused a huge **sinkhole** to open up in the town. It nearly swallowed a small boy.

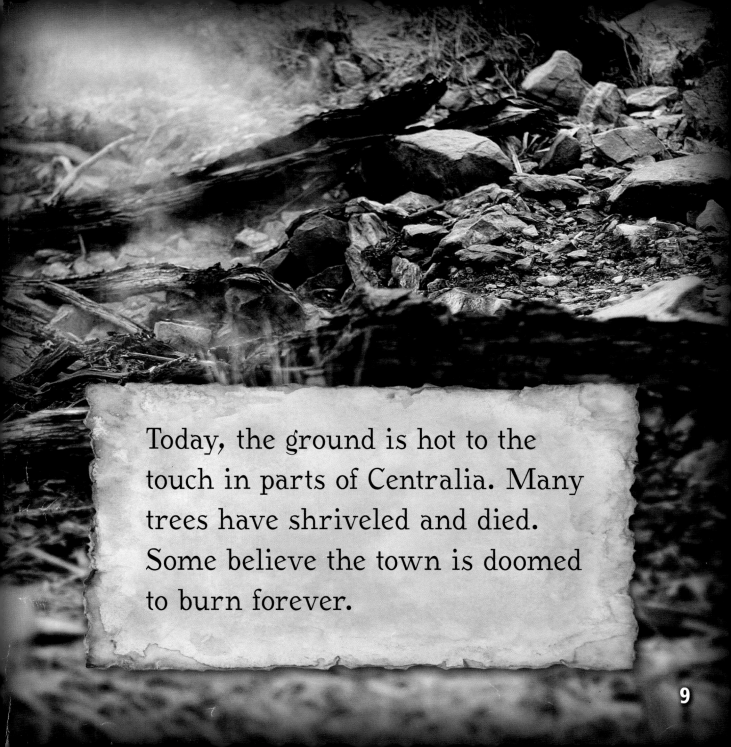

Today, the ground is hot to the touch in parts of Centralia. Many trees have shriveled and died. Some believe the town is doomed to burn forever.

A Wicked Sheriff

Bannack, Montana

A restless spirit is said to haunt the **abandoned** town of Bannack. Could it be the ghost of the town's **infamous** sheriff?

In 1862, gold was found near Bannack. The discovery drew thousands of people—and a wave of crime. To fight the crime, the townspeople chose a new sheriff, Henry Plummer. Unfortunately, he had a secret, evil past.

After Henry became sheriff, crime only got worse. Hundreds were found dead. Henry was thought to be the leader of a gang of murderers! In 1864, he was hanged by an angry mob. Today, his ghost is said to wander Bannack's empty streets.

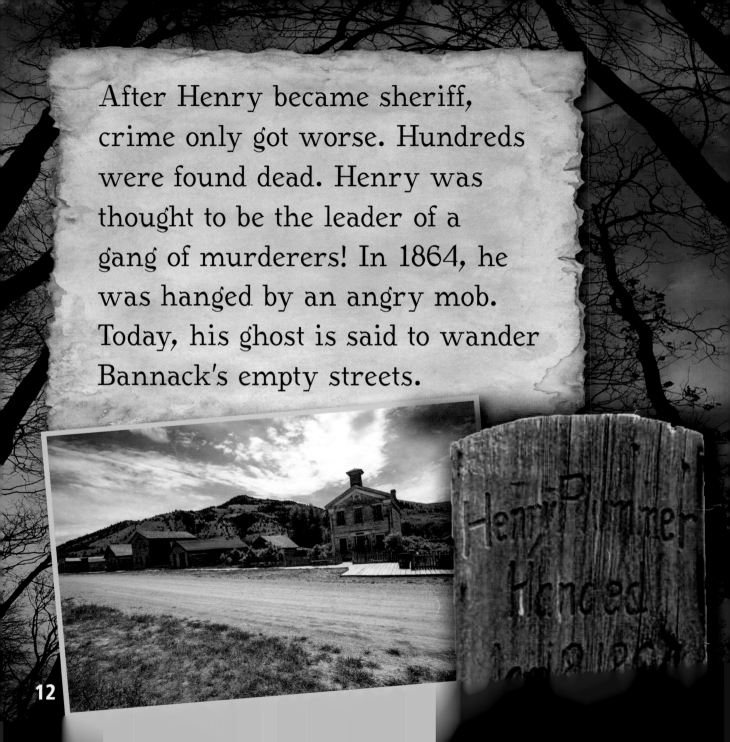

13

The Village of Death

Llanellen, Wales

In the 1600s, a ship sank off the coast of Wales. Most of the crew died in the icy waters. However, a few survived. They were then rescued by the villagers of Llanellen.

The ruins of an old farmhouse in Llanellen

The villagers tried to nurse the sailors. But the men soon died. Then, one by one, all of the villagers got sick and died, too. The sailors had given them the **plague**! After that, the town fell into ruin.

The plague is a deadly disease. It can kill a person within 24 hours.

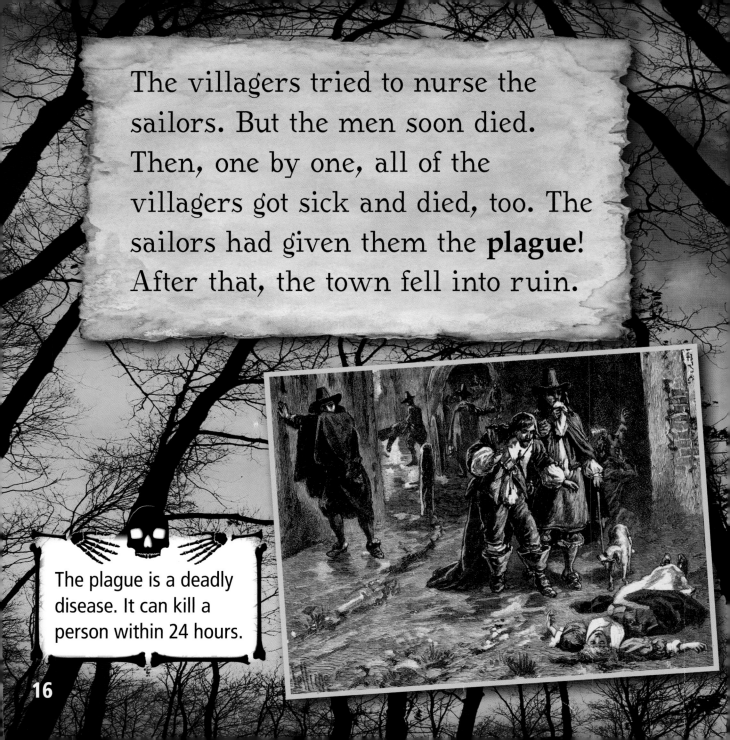

On stormy nights near Llanellen, a woman in white has been seen sobbing. Perhaps she is crying for all those who died.

17

An Eerie Orb

Old Cahawba, Alabama

Old Cahawba was once the **capital** of Alabama. It's now the most famous ghost town in the South. Many people have seen strange things there . . . things that cannot be explained.

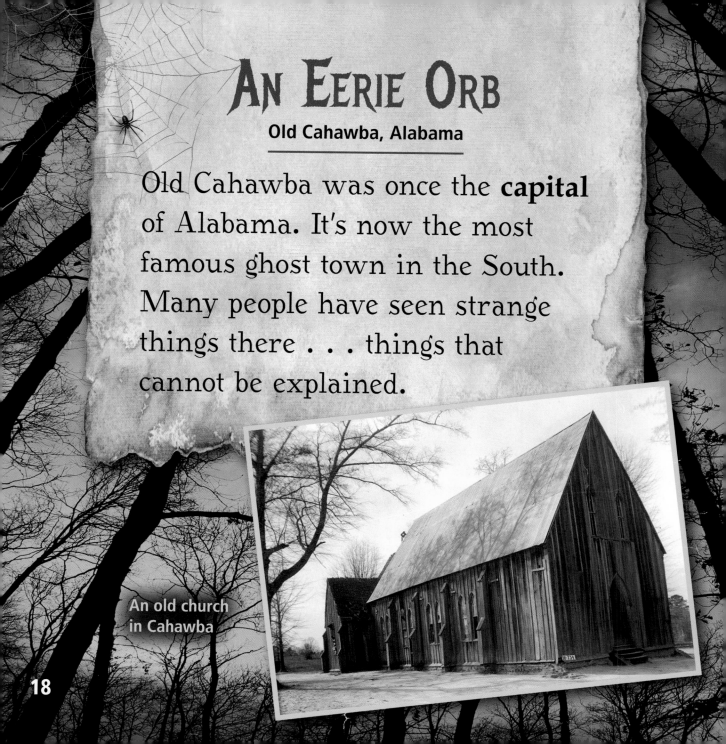

An old church in Cahawba

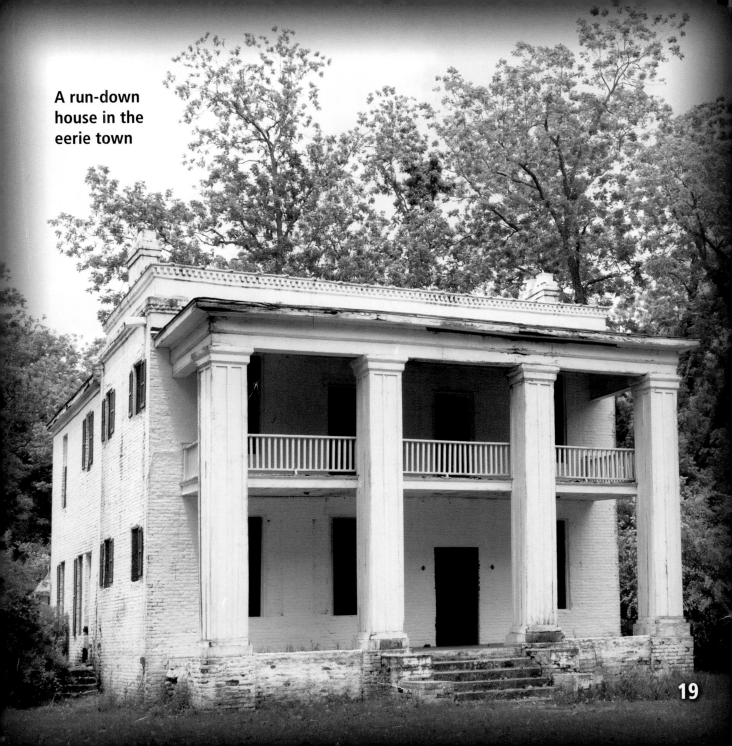

A run-down house in the eerie town

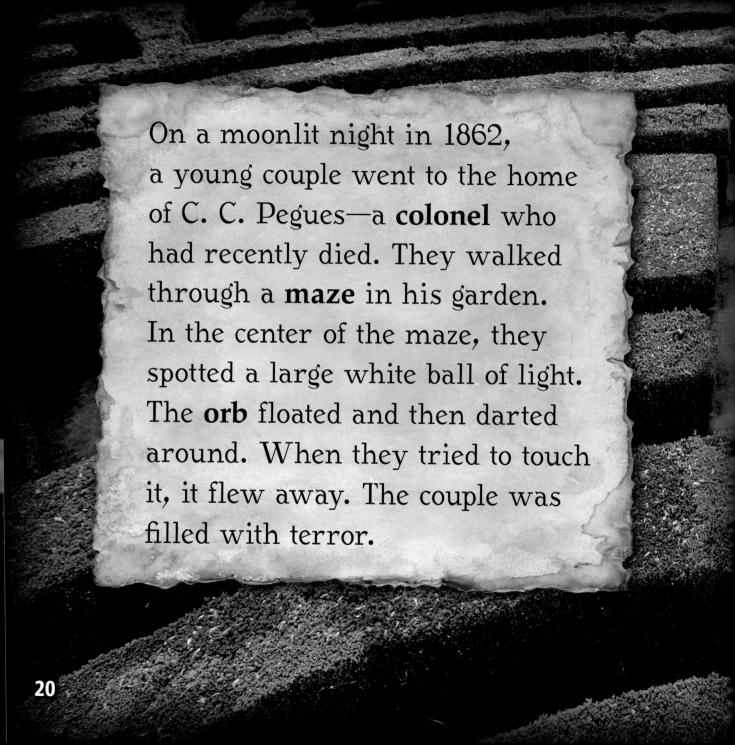

On a moonlit night in 1862, a young couple went to the home of C. C. Pegues—a **colonel** who had recently died. They walked through a **maze** in his garden. In the center of the maze, they spotted a large white ball of light. The **orb** floated and then darted around. When they tried to touch it, it flew away. The couple was filled with terror.

Since that night, many have reported seeing the same white orb. Could it be the lost spirit of Colonel Pegues?

The town has been struck by lightning hundreds of times. Some call it the curse of Cahawba.

GHOSTLY TOWNS
AROUND THE WORLD

BANNACK, MONTANA

Learn the spooky story of this haunted mining town.

CENTRALIA, PENNSYLVANIA

Check out an eerie town that's forever in flames!

OLD CAHAWBA, ALABAMA

Come see a dancing orb and a town forgotten by time.

LLANELLEN, WALES

Visit the site of an old village haunted by death!

Arctic Ocean

NORTH AMERICA

EUROPE

ASIA

Pacific Ocean

Atlantic Ocean

Pacific Ocean

AFRICA

SOUTH AMERICA

Atlantic Ocean

Indian Ocean

AUSTRALIA

Southern Ocean

ANTARCTICA

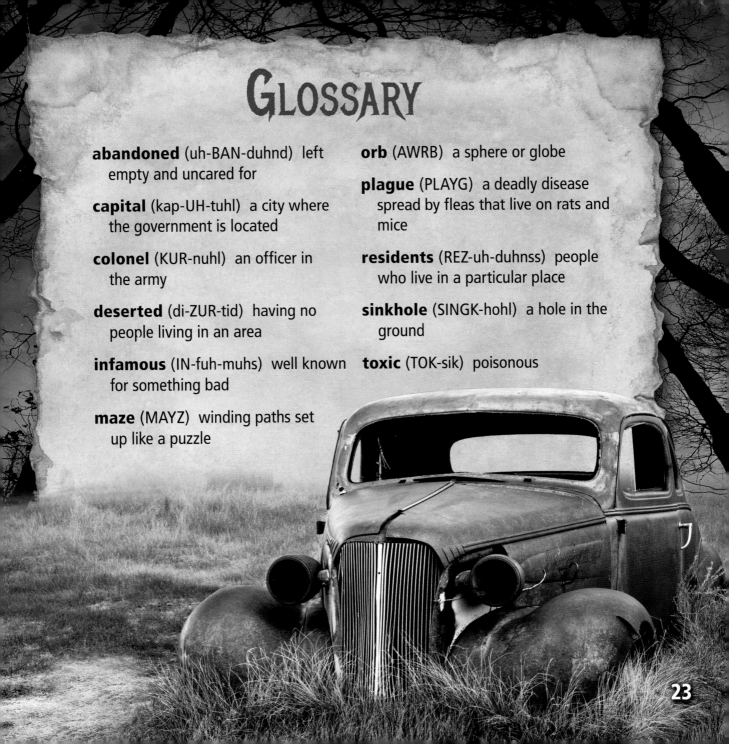

GLOSSARY

abandoned (uh-BAN-duhnd) left empty and uncared for

capital (kap-UH-tuhl) a city where the government is located

colonel (KUR-nuhl) an officer in the army

deserted (di-ZUR-tid) having no people living in an area

infamous (IN-fuh-muhs) well known for something bad

maze (MAYZ) winding paths set up like a puzzle

orb (AWRB) a sphere or globe

plague (PLAYG) a deadly disease spread by fleas that live on rats and mice

residents (REZ-uh-duhnss) people who live in a particular place

sinkhole (SINGK-hohl) a hole in the ground

toxic (TOK-sik) poisonous

Index

Read More

Blake, Kevin. *Bodie: The Town That Belongs to Ghosts (Abandoned! Towns Without People).* New York: Bearport (2015).

Teitelbaum, Michael. *Terror at the Ghost Town Mine (Cold Whispers).* New York: Bearport (2016).

Learn More Online

To learn more about ghostly towns, visit:
www.bearportpublishing.com/Tiptoe

About the Author

Joyce Markovics lives in a 160-year-old house.
Chances are a few otherworldly beings live there, too.